A Note From Denise Renner

The Word of God is so powerful in our lives. It is essential that every person spend time with God and study His Word in order to stay spiritually strong in these last days.

This study guide corresponds to my *TIME With Denise Renner* TV program by the same title that can be viewed at **deniserenner.org**. My desire is that through these lessons, you find the encouragement and freedom in Christ that you need. I believe the Holy Spirit is going to speak to you through the words you read in this study tool and that as you begin to use it, you will be *propelled* into the abundant life God has planned for you. I encourage you to make the effort to receive all He has for you and all He wants to do in you — it will definitely be worth it!

Whether you have walked with the Lord a long time or have just begun to follow Him, there is so much He wants to give you from His Word. He sees where you are, and He wants to meet you there.

> Therefore do not worry about tomorrow, for tomorrow
> will worry about its own things.
> Sufficient for the day is its own trouble.
> — Matthew 6:34

Your sister and friend in Jesus Christ,

Denise Renner

Faith Will Be Your Anchor in the Storm

Copyright © 2025 by Denise Renner
1814 W. Tacoma St.
Broken Arrow, OK 74012-1406

Published by Rick Renner Ministries
www.renner.org

ISBN 13: 978-1-6675-1341-6

ISBN 13 eBook: 978-1-6675-1342-3

TOPIC

How Will You Survive the Storm?

SCRIPTURES

1. **Mark 4:35-40** — On the same day, when evening had come, He said to them, "Let us cross over to the other side." Now when they had left the multitude, they took Him along in the boat as He was. And other little boats were also with Him. And a great windstorm arose, and the waves beat into the boat, so that it was already filling. But He was in the stern, asleep on a pillow. And they awoke Him and said to Him, "Teacher, do You not care that we are perishing?" Then He arose and rebuked the wind, and said to the sea, "Peace, be still!" And the wind ceased and there was a great calm. But He said to them, "Why are you so fearful? How is it that you have no faith?"

2. **Proverbs 4:23** — Keep your heart with all diligence, for out of it spring the issues of life.

3. **Proverbs 4:25** — Let your eyes look straight ahead, and your eyelids look right before you.

4. **Philippians 3:12-13** — Not that I have already attained, or am already perfected; but I press on, that I may lay hold of that for which Christ Jesus has also laid hold of me. Brethren, I do not count myself to have apprehended; but one thing I do, forgetting those things which are behind and reaching forward to those things which are ahead.

5. **Hebrews 13:8** — Jesus Christ is the same yesterday, today, and forever.

6. **Proverbs 4:25-26** — Let your eyes look straight ahead, and your eyelids look right before you. Ponder the path of your feet, and let all your ways be established.

7. **Hebrews 10:38-39** — Now the just shall live by faith; but if anyone draws back, my soul has no pleasure in him. But we are not of those who draw back to perdition, but of those who believe to the saving of the soul.

8. **Isaiah 41:10,13** — "'Fear not, for I am with you; Be not dismayed, for I am your God. I will strengthen you, Yes, I will help you, I will

uphold you with My righteous right hand.' For I, the Lord your God, will hold your right hand...."

9. **Hebrews 12:2** — Looking unto Jesus, the author and finisher of our faith....

SYNOPSIS

The five lessons in this study on *Faith Will Be Your Anchor in the Storm* will focus on the following topics:

- How Will You Survive the Storm?
- Is Your Faith Persistent?
- Does Your Faith Have a Goal?
- What Can Faith Do?
- How Can You Get to Jesus?

The emphasis of this lesson:

During the storm, the disciples panicked, but Jesus stayed in peace. When we face storms in life, we must guard our heart and draw strength from the Greater One living inside us. Jesus will enable us to ignore the devil, forget the past, and focus on the future, so we can finish what He's called us to do.

The Disciples Were Thrust Into a Life-Threatening Storm

Storms are a part of life that come to every person. Because this is unavoidable, the question you may ask is, "What am I to do when I'm in a storm?" To answer this, we will turn to the story of the disciples and the massive storm they faced while out on the Sea of Galilee. The Bible says:

> **On the same day, when evening had come, He [Jesus] said to them, "Let us cross over to the other side."**
> **— Mark 4:35**

The most important part of this verse is that Jesus told the disciples what was going to happen beforehand. He declared, "We're crossing over to the other side."

You might be in a stormy situation right now and it may feel like the wind is blowing and the waves are crashing against you. Difficult — even life-threatening — reports may be coming your way regarding your finances, your health, or the health of a loved one. But if Jesus has promised you that you're going "to the other side" of the situation, then you're going to make it to the other side. You have His Word on it!

In Mark 4:36 and 37, the Bible goes on to say:

> **Now when they had left the multitude, they took Him along in the boat as He was. And other little boats were also with Him. And a great windstorm arose, and the waves beat into the boat, so that it was already filling.**

Obviously, when a boat is filling with water, that means it is going down. So this tells us this storm was serious and life-threatening to Jesus and His disciples. It is safe to say the disciples had many questions racing through their minds such as, *Why did I get on this boat with Jesus? Are we going to survive this storm? Am I ever going to see my family again?*

Jesus Was at Peace and Took Control of the Storm

Have you ever been in a catastrophic situation like that where the emotional and mental pressures were palpable? Have you ever faced something so overwhelming that it seemed as though everything was closing in around you? That is the type of situation the disciples found themselves in. But Jesus had already said, "We're crossing over to the other side."

As the great windstorm arose, and the waves beat into the boat so intensely that it was already filling with water, Scripture says:

> **But He [Jesus] was in the stern, asleep on a pillow. And they awoke Him and said to Him, "Teacher, do You not care that we are perishing?"**
> **— Mark 4:38**

Amazingly, in the midst of what is understood to have been hurricane force winds, Jesus was in such a state of peace that He was able to sleep. Not so with the disciples. They were in so much fear and anxiety that they panicked and woke Jesus up. Their actions show that they didn't believe what Jesus had said — that they were going to make it to the other side — and their words demonstrated that they didn't believe He cared.

How often is that also our story? We may be going through things in which there seems to be no way out, and we're tempted to say, "Where are You, Lord? I am about to go under. Don't you even care?" That's exactly what the disciples said.

In Mark 4:39 and 40, the Bible says:

> Then He [Jesus] arose and rebuked the wind, and said to the sea, "Peace, be still!" And the wind ceased and there was a great calm. But He said to them, "Why are you so fearful? How is it that you have no faith?"

Basically, Jesus told His disciples, "Why are you so afraid? Couldn't you believe Me? Couldn't you trust what I said — that we're going to the other side? How can it be that after all you have seen Me do that you have no faith?"

Guard Your Heart Diligently

Now you may be thinking, *What can I do to make it through life's storms?* An important answer to this question is found in Proverbs 4:23, which says:

> Keep your heart with all diligence, for out of it spring the issues of life.

There's so much that goes on in our heart, and when we're in a stormy situation, one of the first things that tries to enter and take over is fear. When we look at the wind and the waves, we begin to hear thoughts like, *What if this happens or that happens? How in the world am I going to make it? And what does my future hold?*

Question after question bombards our mind, and those thoughts do not usually lead us in the direction of peace. Instead of stilling the storm, this internal interrogation causes the storm inside us to intensify. In this fearful mindset, we begin to believe, *The one that is in the world is greater than the One living in me. The one on the outside pushing all the buttons and bringing all the pressure against me is the greater one.*

But those thoughts are lies from Satan, who is the father of lies (*see* John 8:44).

The Greater One Lives in You

The One on the *inside* of you — the Holy Spirit — *is far greater* than any pressure that's on the outside! Yes, pressures come, and they may cause your mind not to think right or your emotions to be all stirred up in an unhealthy way. But that doesn't change the fact that the Greater One lives inside your spirit. The Bible declares:

> **You are of God, little children, and have overcome them, because He who is in you is greater than he who is in the world.**
> **— 1 John 4:4**

If you will focus on your spirit where faith is, you can guard your heart. You can pray, "Lord, I know I may not be thinking the right thoughts right now or feeling the right emotions. But You are living inside of me, and You are my strength. Release Your power in me to go through this storm. Release Your power in me to boldly say, 'Get out of my way, devil. I'm not listening to your thoughts. Emotions, be quiet. I'm going to listen to God's Word hidden on the inside of my heart.' I ask this in Jesus' name."

Friend, this is your part in guarding your heart. The Bible says you are to hide God's Word in your heart and keep your heart with all diligence, for out of it spring the issues of life (*see* Psalm 119:11; Proverbs 4:23). Keeping your heart is not your pastor's job, your spouse's job, or your friend's job. They can't keep your heart. That is your responsibility, and if you listen and stay tuned to the Greater One living in you, He will help you do just that.

Focus on the Future, Not on the Past

In Proverbs 4:25, Solomon says, "Let your eyes look straight ahead, and your eyelids look right before you." Oh, what an important reminder. When you're in a fight, let your eyes stay focused on what is straight ahead — to complete the task God has called you to do.

That is what the apostle Paul did even when he was locked up in a horrible prison. In Philippians 3:12 he candidly shared these amazing words:

> **Not that I have already attained, or am already perfected; but I press on, that I may lay hold of that for which Christ Jesus has also laid hold of me.**

This was Paul's attitude in the storm he was facing. He had not yet completed all the tasks that Jesus had given him to do, yet he knew he was to press on to the finish line. How about you? Have you finished doing everything God has called you to do? If you haven't, then you need to press on, keep laying hold of the power of God, and push through that storm to get to the other side.

In Philippians 3:13, Paul went on to say:

> **Brethren, I do not count myself to have apprehended; but one thing I do, forgetting those things which are behind and reaching forward to those things which are ahead.**

Notice Paul made a decision to forget the things that were behind him. That is important because when you're in a storm, sometimes the past can begin speaking to you through your thoughts. The devil will say things like, "You know how you reacted last time you were in a storm. It was so bad, and you didn't make it through. I don't think you're going to get through this one either. Let's face it, you're weak and you lack the character to endure."

Again, the devil is a liar, so don't listen to him. Say and do what Paul did: "...Forgetting those things which are behind and reaching forward to those things which are ahead, I press toward the goal for the prize of the upward call of God in Christ Jesus" (Philippians 3:13-14).

What is ahead for you and me? The promises of God that are yet to be fulfilled in our lives. Remember, "Jesus Christ is the same yesterday, today, and forever" (Hebrews 13:8). Circumstances and situations will change, your emotions will change, and your thinking will probably change, but Jesus will never change. He is *rock solid*. And when we put our faith in Him, we will be strengthened by Him — our Mighty Rock that never moves.

Walk by Faith and Don't Be Shaken by Fear

Again, God's Word instructs us, "Let your eyes look straight ahead, and your eyelids look right before you. Ponder the path of your feet, and let all your ways be established" (Proverbs 4:25-26). It is so important to have your focus on what's in front of you and have a resolve in your heart that you're not going to be moved by your circumstances.

Of course, this doesn't happen automatically. It happens when we choose daily to walk by faith and not by sight. The writer of Hebrews makes this clear in Hebrews 10:38 and 39:

Now the just shall live by faith; but if anyone draws back, my soul has no pleasure in him. But we are not of those who draw back to perdition, but of those who believe to the saving of the soul.

That's our destination — the saving of our soul. We must keep believing and keep emphasizing what we know is true in our spirit — that the very Spirit of Jesus is inside us, the Holy Spirit, who is the Third Person of the Godhead. He has taken up permanent residence in us. He gives us His mighty power to believe His Word and to trust Him to do what He has said!

Friend, God is not backing away from His promises. He's waiting for us to take Him at His Word and believe. In fact, He's given us every reason to believe and not be afraid. In Isaiah 41:10 and 13, He declares:

"Fear not, for I am with you; Be not dismayed, for I am your God. I will strengthen you, yes, I will help you, I will uphold you with My righteous right hand." For I, the Lord your God, will hold your right hand….

Aren't you grateful that God holds us by His right hand! If we will keep holding on to Him and cooperating with the work of His Holy Spirit, He will bring about the saving of our soul.

The Bible also says in Hebrews 12:2 that we are to keep our eyes fixed on "…Jesus, the author and finisher of our faith…." He is the One keeping us. He's the Author, which means He started the work in our hearts, and He is the Finisher. So, from the start of the timeline of our journey with Him to the end, He's right there with us.

Friend, if you're in a storm, God is right there in your boat with you. Just reach out and call to Him and say, "Lord, help me," and His presence is there. His Holy Spirit is the great Helper, the great Comforter, the great Teacher, and the great Guide. He will uphold His reputation and will come to your aid when you call Him!

STUDY QUESTIONS

> Be diligent to present yourself approved to God, a worker
> who does not need to be ashamed, rightly dividing the word of truth.
> — 2 Timothy 2:15

1. One of the most important things to remember in a storm is that the Greater One is living in you. The moment you were saved, the Holy Spirit moved into your heart and took up permanent residency. To drive this truth deep into your heart, look up these passages and write down what the Holy Spirit shows you about this powerful reality.
   * John 14:16-17, 23
   * Romans 8:11
   * Galatians 4:6
   * First John 3:24; 4:13
   * First Corinthians 3:16; 6:19; Second Corinthians 6:16

2. To make it through the storms of life, *strong faith* is a must-have. We need faith to trust Jesus to keep His Word and carry us through. What does the Bible say in these verses about your faith being built and strengthened?
   * Psalm 18:1-3; 27:1; 28:7-8; 118:14
   * Romans 10:17; Acts 20:32
   * Romans 4:19-20
   * Jude 20; First Corinthians 14:4

PRACTICAL APPLICATION

> But be doers of the word,
> and not hearers only, deceiving yourselves.
> — James 1:22

1. Are you in a stormy situation right now? Do you feel as though the wind is blowing and the waves are crashing against you? Take a few moments to briefly describe what you are experiencing.

2. What are your greatest worries and fears regarding the difficulty you're facing? Take those cares and concerns to God in prayer and cast them on Him (*see* 1 Peter 5:7; Psalm 34:4; 62:8). As you give Him

all your anxieties and worries, He will give you His peace to make it through the storm (*see* Philippians 4:6-8).

TOPIC

Is Your Faith Persistent?

SCRIPTURES

1. **Mark 5:25-26** — Now a certain woman had a flow of blood for twelve years, and had suffered many things from many physicians. She had spent all that she had and was no better, but rather grew worse.

2. **Hebrews 11:27** — By faith he forsook Egypt, not fearing the wrath of the king; for he endured as seeing Him who is invisible.

3. **Matthew 15:22-28** — And behold, a woman of Canaan came from that region and cried out to Him, saying, "Have mercy on me, O Lord, Son of David! My daughter is severely demon-possessed." But He answered her not a word. And His disciples came and urged Him, saying, "Send her away, for she cries out after us." But He answered and said, "I was not sent except to the lost sheep of the house of Israel." Then she came and worshiped Him, saying, "Lord, help me!" But He answered and said, "It is not good to take the children's bread and throw it to the little dogs." And she said, "Yes, Lord, yet even the little dogs eat the crumbs which fall from their masters' table." Then Jesus answered and said to her, "O woman, great is your faith! Let it be to you as you desire." And her daughter was healed from that very hour.

4. **1 John 5:4** — For whatever is born of God overcomes the world. And this is the victory that has overcome the world — our faith.

SYNOPSIS

We saw in Lesson 1 that storms are a part of life, and they come in many forms. Sometimes the storm we face is financial, and other times, it is sickness and disease. This is what the Canaanite woman from the region of Tyre and Sidon was facing. But because she had a never-give-up kind of faith, she received exactly what she was seeking from Jesus — healing for her daughter.

The emphasis of this lesson:

A Canaanite woman with a severely demon-possessed daughter sought Jesus for healing. Knowing He was her only hope, she pushed past all obstacles and humbly worshipped Jesus. Through her persistent faith, she received the healing for her daughter she needed.

Realizing That Jesus Is Our Only Answer Causes Persistent Faith To Develop

The enemy uses many things in life to try to stop us. Mistreatment and abuse from others, worry and fear, offense and unforgiveness, and the negative opinions of others are all ammo in his arsenal to overwhelm us and get us to quit. But through Christ and faith in God's Word, we can become *unstoppable!* We can develop a persistent kind of faith like that of the Canaanite woman who would not give up until she got what she needed from Jesus.

Many people who have had a sickness or disease have gone to doctors to try to get well, but even after receiving all the medicines and treatments offered, they didn't get any better. That is what happened to the woman with the issue of blood. The Bible says, "…[She] had suffered many things from many physicians. She had spent all that she had and was no better, but rather grew worse" (Mark 5:26). Her problem was severe, and the only real answer she had was Jesus.

Coming to this realization about Jesus is vital for the development of our faith. If we think that we can get an answer from some other person or place, then we'll seek after those things because they're something we can easily see and touch. But when nothing in the natural realm will work, we are forced to believe in what we cannot see, which is God and His Word.

That is what Moses did. Hebrews 11:27 says, "By faith he [Moses] forsook Egypt, not fearing the wrath of the king; for he endured as seeing Him who is invisible." Thus, the reason Moses was able to make it through so many trials was because he was focused on God who is invisible.

For the Canaanite woman whose daughter was demon-possessed, she knew who the answer was and what the answer wasn't. She had come to the conclusion that only Jesus could provide the delivering power her daughter needed. Hence, she pursued Him and was not willing to stop until she received her answer.

A Canaanite Woman
Came To Jesus for Healing

Our story opens in Matthew's gospel, where he wrote:

> **And behold, a woman of Canaan came from that region and cried out to Him, saying, "Have mercy on me, O Lord, Son of David! My daughter is severely demon-possessed."**
> **— Matthew 15:22**

From the start, you need to know that the Canaanites had been arch enemies with Israel, which means this woman already had a major strike against her by virtue of her nationality. She knew that her family's ancestry could possibly be a hindrance for her coming to Jesus, but she didn't care about that. She believed that He was her only answer, so she continued in her pursuit of her daughter's healing and deliverance.

Although Scripture doesn't specifically say how she learned about Jesus, it is safe to say she must have heard testimonies of what He had done in the lives of others. Why else would she have cried out to Him? It wasn't because of His clothes, His hair, or His friends. Maybe one of her friends had received their healing from Jesus — or maybe someone's relative was delivered from demons. Whatever the case, she somehow became aware of Jesus' supernatural power to heal and deliver, which is why she sought after Him.

Something else that is significant about Matthew 15:22 is that it says this woman's daughter was *severely* demon-possessed. Although there are other demon-possessed people in the Scriptures, no one else is described like this. We know of:

- A demon-possessed man screaming (*see* Mark 1:23-25).
- A demon-possessed man cutting himself (*see* Mark 5:1-5).
- Two demon-possessed men living in tombs (*see* Matthew 8:28).
- A demon-possessed boy who was foaming at the mouth (*see* Mark 9:17-20).

- A demon-possessed boy who was often thrown into fire and water (*see* Matthew 17:14-18).

These are all horrible situations. Can you imagine having a child with those kinds of problems? That is what this Canaanite woman was dealing with. She loved her daughter dearly, but her daughter was severely demon-possessed.

What exactly did it look like to be "severely possessed by demons"? We don't know, but it must have been quite challenging. Did this mom sleep at night? Was she worried? Was her hair falling out or her stomach filled with ulcers because of what her daughter was dealing with? Had she lost all her money on treatments? Was she mean to people because of the stress she was dealing with?

The Bible doesn't give us the details, but this was a real situation with a real mother and a real demon-possessed daughter. Hence, when the Canaanite woman saw Jesus and heard of His delivering power, she knew He was her answer.

She Was Ignored, Rejected, and Insulted

Looking again at Matthew 15:22, it says, "And behold, a woman of Canaan came from that region and cried out to Him, saying, 'Have mercy on me, O Lord, Son of David! My daughter is severely demon-possessed.'"

What was Jesus' response to this woman's desperate plea? The Bible says:

But He answered her not a word. And His disciples came and urged Him, saying, "Send her away, for she cries out after us."
— Matthew 15:23

Amazingly, Jesus just ignored this woman, and to make matters worse, His disciples came and urged Him to have her removed from their presence because her hysterical crying was a nuisance. Clearly, that was not the response she was hoping for. What she wanted was for Jesus to have mercy on her and bring healing to her daughter.

What happened next? Matthew 15:24 says:

But He answered and said, "I was not sent except to the lost sheep of the house of Israel."

This was Jesus' way of saying, "I'm not trying to ignore you, but I was not sent to the Canaanites. It is not my place to come to you. I was sent by My Father to the lost sheep of Israel."

Yet, She Humbled Herself and Worshipped Jesus

Undeterred by Jesus' response and the rejection of His disciples, the Bible says this Canaanite woman "...came and worshiped Him, saying, 'Lord, help me!'" (Matthew 15:25).

So what did her worship look like? Was she on the ground? Was she touching his feet? Did she say things like, "Lord, I worship You! You're my only answer. You're the son of David, and I worship you. Lord, you're the only one who can help me, and I worship you. You are my answer."

Some people think worship is raising our hands and maybe singing, and while that is certainly a part of worship, there's more to it than that. In worship, there's *an exchange*. It's a place of humility where we come before God and say, "Lord, I don't have the answers. Only You do. I'm not Lord and I'm not Savior — You are. I am Your sheep and You are my Shepherd."

Friend, that is worship. It is laying down our pride and exchanging it for Jesus' humility. Instead of thinking, *I'm so wonderful, and I can do this on my own*, worship God and declare, "You are wonderful! And I can't do this without You. You're the only one who can help me, Lord...You are my answer, and I surrender to You, my Lord and my Savior."

The Bible says this Canaanite woman worshipped Jesus, and after she worshipped Him, she prayed a short prayer. It was a three-word, non-religious prayer, and it was very powerful. She simply said, "Lord, help me."

Healing Is the 'Children's Bread'

What was Jesus' response to this woman's worship and prayer? Matthew 15:26 says:

> **But He answered and said, "It is not good to take the children's bread and throw it to the little dogs."**

This answer from Jesus may seem surprising, but it also has great significance. This is the first time in Scripture that we see "healing" called *the children's bread*.

Think about it. Bread is a common item on a kitchen table and a basic essential, which tells us healing should also be "on the table" and easily accessible for those who come to Jesus. He has made healing readily available, like bread on the table.

In this case, however, Jesus told the Canaanite woman that the bread of healing was *not* for her because she was not one of the children of Israel. But that did not stop her. She knew in her heart that Jesus was the only answer for her daughter's healing.

Maintaining a posture of humble worship, the woman replied:

> …**"Yes, Lord, yet even the little dogs eat the crumbs which fall from their masters' table."**
> **— Matthew 15:27**

In her response, you can almost hear her say, "Okay, You're calling me a little dog, but that's okay. You're also calling healing *bread*, and bread on the table always has crumbs that fall on the floor. Even the dogs under the table are allowed to eat the crumbs, so since I'm a little dog, I will take some of those crumbs, Lord! I don't have to have a whole loaf of bread. Just give me a tiny crumb, and in that crumb is all the delivering power my daughter needs!"

Jesus Marveled at Her Great Faith

This woman was not giving up, and Jesus marveled at her tenacity. He answered her and said:

> …**"O woman, great is your faith! Let it be to you as you desire."**
> **And her daughter was healed from that very hour.**
> **— Matthew 15:28**

Up until this moment, things were not looking good for this Canaanite woman and her daughter. The disciples wanted to silence her, and Jesus seemed to ignore her. He basically said to her, "The bread of healing is not for you."

Every single door this woman knocked on seemed to be slammed in her face. But when Jesus likened healing to bread, she decided to put herself in the humble position of "a little dog" and be more than willing to receive the crumbs of healing that fell from His table.

Something happened in this woman's heart when she worshipped Jesus. Her faith became more aggressive. Likewise, if you want your faith to increase, make that exchange! Humble yourself in worship and say, "Lord, if I'm proud and if I think I can do this on my own, I repent. You are my only answer, Lord, and I worship *You!*" When you worship Jesus like that, it increases your faith.

Friend, you would be wise to pay attention to the faith God put on the inside of you when you were born again. It is through that faith you overcome the world (*see* 1 John 5:4). So hold on to the promises of God's Word no matter what your situation looks like. Be like the Canaanite woman. Worship the Lord and trust Him. Believe He is who He says He is and that He'll do what He said He would do. God is attentive to that kind of faith!

STUDY QUESTIONS

Be diligent to present yourself approved to God, a worker who does not need to be ashamed, rightly dividing the word of truth.
— 2 Timothy 2:15

1. *Humility* is vital to receiving what we need from God, and this Canaanite woman's life demonstrates this. How important and powerful is humility in God's eyes? Study these passages and write what you learn:

    • What happens when you choose humility? *See* Proverbs 3:34; James 4:6; First Peter 5:5-6.

    • What are some of the blessings of humility? *See* Proverbs 22:4; 29:23; Matthew 18:4.

    • How did Jesus model humility, and how does it apply to you? *See* Matthew 16:24-27; Philippians 2:3-11.

2. In the story of the Canaanite woman, it seems that every door she knocked on was slammed in her face — until the very end. Have you felt that way with what you are asking God to do in your life? Take time to learn what Jesus said about being persistent in prayer:

    • Keep on praying — Matthew 7:7-11; Luke 11:9-13; John 14:13-14

    • Persistence pays off — Luke 11:5-8; Luke 18:1-8

    What is the Holy Spirit speaking to you in these passages?

PRACTICAL APPLICATION

But be doers of the word,
and not hearers only, deceiving yourselves.
—James 1:22

1. In this lesson, we've explored the story of the Canaanite woman and her persistent faith to receive healing for her daughter from Jesus. Is there something you are now seeing that you have not seen before in this story? How does it apply to your own life?

2. Instead of being offended by Jesus' response, the Canaanite woman humbled herself and began to worship Him (*see* Matthew 15:25). What do the words "worshipping God" mean to you? How do you express *your* worship to God — and what does worship look like in your life?

LESSON 3

TOPIC

Does Your Faith Have a Goal?

SCRIPTURES

1. **1 John 5:4** — For whatever is born of God overcomes the world. And this is the victory that has overcome the world — our faith.

2. **Ephesians 1:19** — And what is the exceeding greatness of His power toward us who believe, according to the working of His mighty power.

3. **Mark 5:25-34** — Now a certain woman had a flow of blood for twelve years, and had suffered many things from many physicians. She had spent all that she had and was no better, but rather grew worse. When she heard about Jesus, she came behind Him in the crowd and touched His garment. For she said, "If only I may touch His clothes, I shall be made well." Immediately the fountain of her blood was dried up, and she felt in her body that she was healed of the affliction. And Jesus, immediately knowing in Himself that power had gone out of Him, turned around in the crowd and said, "Who touched My clothes?" But His disciples said to Him, "You see the multitude thronging You, and You say, 'Who touched Me?'" And He looked

around to see her who had done this thing. But the woman, fearing and trembling, knowing what had happened to her, came and fell down before Him and told Him the whole truth. And He said to her, "Daughter, your faith has made you well. Go in peace, and be healed of your affliction."

4. **Ephesians 1:19-21** — And what is the exceeding greatness of His power toward us who believe, according to the working of His mighty power which He worked in Christ when He raised Him from the dead and seated Him at His right hand in the heavenly places, far above all principality and power and might and dominion, and every name that is named, not only in this age but also in that which is to come.

SYNOPSIS

As a born-again child of God, you were given a measure of faith by God Himself the moment you repented of your sin and invited Jesus to be your Savior and Lord. That living faith was deposited within you, and it serves as an anchor for you in any storm you face. The key to activating this anchor is knowing God's Word and learning how to aim your faith at a specific target. This is what the woman with the issue of blood did as we will see in this lesson.

The emphasis of this lesson:

The woman with the issue of blood had a laser-focused faith. She pursued Jesus tenaciously and received the healing she needed. Persistent faith is praised and rewarded by Jesus, so do whatever you need to do to get to Him and experience the greatness of His power.

Jesus' Pain Had a Purpose

The gospels are full of the stories of miracles and healings that Jesus did throughout His ministry. As wonderful and powerful as those things are that took place, even though we read about them and study them, if all we do is learn about them in the Bible but we never see any miracles with our own eyes, those things can seem like a mere fairytale to us.

What we must realize is that Jesus paid a very high price for us to experience His manifest presence, His healing, and His miracle-working power in our own lives. God is not dead — He is alive! And the miracles and healings He did through Jesus then He is still doing now! His supernatural power is not confined to history or the heavenly realm. On the contrary, "…The exceeding greatness of His power [is moving] toward us who believe, according to the working of His mighty power" (Ephesians 1:19).

Friend, our Heavenly Father is full of compassion, mercy, and love toward us. There is nothing in Him that wants you to be sick or tormented by the enemy mentally or emotionally. Jesus paid for your healing and wholeness through the horrific torture He suffered in His own body. Isaiah 53:4-5 says:

> **Surely He has borne our griefs and carried our sorrows; Yet we esteemed Him stricken, smitten by God, and afflicted. But He was wounded for our transgressions, He was bruised for our iniquities; the chastisement for our peace was upon Him, and by His stripes we are healed.**

What Jesus suffered was not in vain. All the abuse and the torture He endured had a purpose — to redeem *us* from sickness and disease! He took our pain, our shame, our sickness, and our disease into His own body. Every drop of blood He shed from the Garden of Gethsemane to the cross of Calvary was for your salvation, your deliverance, your peace of mind, your joy, and your healing. Praise His mighty Name!

12 Years of Suffering and Sorrow

There is a woman talked about in three of the four gospels — Matthew, Mark, and Luke. Her story demonstrates a laser-focused faith that caused her to receive what she needed from Jesus. Like the Canaanite woman we talked about in Lesson 2, this woman also had somehow and at some point, heard testimonies of Jesus' healing power. Her story begins with these words:

> **Now a certain woman had a flow of blood for twelve years.**
> **— Mark 5:25**

Can you imagine your body constantly bleeding for 12 years? This woman must have lived so physically weak and exhausted every day from this situation. Not to mention the emotional and mental trauma she had to endure all those years from being viewed as "unclean" in the eyes of Jewish society. In those days, anytime a woman was bleeding, she was considered unclean, and everywhere she sat was also deemed unclean for several days.

If someone touched her, sat where she had sat, or lay where she had lain, they too would be considered unclean for a certain period of time. In fact, anyone who was considered unclean according to Jewish law like this woman with the continual flow of blood was to announce, "Unclean! Unclean!" to warn people around them of contamination if any person touched them.

In addition to being a social outcast, weak, and sick, the Bible says this woman "…had suffered many things from many physicians. She had spent all that she had and was no better, but rather grew worse" (Mark 5:26). If you have ever been sick or dealt with physical or mental challenges for an extended period of time, you know how exhausting and financially draining it can be.

Denise Experienced Suffering and Received God's Divine Healing Power

Denise candidly shared how she could identify with some of the pain that the woman with the issue of blood endured. For 13 years she had a skin disease on her face that would not go away. She had gone to one doctor after another, taking all the medications they prescribed and subjecting herself to all the treatments they recommended. But nothing worked.

"One treatment I'll never forget," Denise said, "was when they put dry ice on my face. It literally burned my skin, causing the sores to form scabs, which they later peeled off. It is hard to describe the pain I went through — not just physically, but mentally and emotionally as well."

"I was in high school for many of those years," Denise continued, "and having to walk the hallways and go to classes with my face looking like the craters of the moon was horrible. In my mind, everyone else was better than me because of how my face looked."

Thankfully, Denise heard the good news of Isaiah 53:5 — that by the stripes of Jesus we are healed. She grabbed hold of that promise, and for two months, she declared it out loud over her skin. In the meantime, while she was waiting and believing for her healing, God showed her some things inside her soul that needed to change, including some unforgiveness that she needed to get rid of.

When Denise let go of the offense she had been holding on to and began praying for the people who hurt her, something changed. She went to bed one night with that disease on her face just like she had done for 13 years. But when she woke up the next morning, her skin was completely clean and clear! Her forehead, her cheeks, and her neck were all blemish-free and no longer swollen.

"I was completely healed by the power of God!" Denise proclaimed. "That's why I have a passion to see other people healed because I know we serve a healing Jesus! If you are suffering with sickness or a disease, I want you to know that Jesus healed me, and He wants to heal you too."

Laser-Focused Faith Obtains What It Seeks

Returning to our story of the woman with the issue of blood, the Bible says that after she had suffered many things from many physicians and had spent all her money, she hadn't gotten any better but rather grew worse (*see* Mark 5:26).

Then somehow she heard testimonies of Jesus' miracle-working power, and a glimmer of hope came alive in her heart. The Scripture says:

> **When she heard about Jesus, she came behind Him in the crowd and touched His garment. For she said, "If only I may touch His clothes, I shall be made well." Immediately the fountain of her blood was dried up, and she felt in her body that she was healed of the affliction.**
>
> **— Mark 5:27-29**

Take a moment to slowly read this passage again and notice how this woman's faith was laser-focused on the healing she was believing for. The intense pain of being ostracized and the desire to be clean again motivated her to press through the crowd and touch Jesus.

Remember, she had been bleeding for 12 years, making her unclean and an outcast to society. Any person and any place she touched became unclean for a period of time. If she had friends, they would have had to keep their distance. If she had a husband, she would have had to abstain from having any type of physical relations with him. Likewise, if she had children, she would have had minimal, if any, contact with them or they, too, would be rendered unclean.

Upon hearing about Jesus' ability to heal and that He was passing through her town, this woman pushed past all the obstacles — including the massive crowd — to get to Jesus. She knew that the people had every right to start screaming, "Unclean! Unclean!" and demean and reject her, but it didn't matter. Her faith was laser-focused on getting through to Jesus and touching His clothes.

Do Whatever You Need To Do To Get to Jesus

Mark 5:28 says, "For she said, 'If only I may touch His clothes, I shall be made well.'" When we study this story in the gospels, we find that this woman doesn't just say this once. Rather, she says it again and again, "If only I may touch His clothes, I shall be made well."

Some scholars say this woman may have been crawling on the ground. Because there were so many people present and everyone was wearing long robes, she was probably able to stay hidden from people's view while she was down there. She stayed laser-focused in her faith, crawling her way closer and closer to Jesus — all the while muttering under her breath, "If only I can touch His clothes, I shall be made well. Just once. All I need to do is push in a little further and touch the hem of His garment, and I know I'm going to be healed."

With every ounce of energy she could muster, she navigated through and around the legs and feet of the multitude pressing in all around her. Her ears were listening for the voice of Jesus, and her eyes scanned the ground to find His feet. Finally, she could see the hem of Jesus' garment, and although she was exhausted, it didn't matter. Her laser-focused faith helped her maintain her forward motion that was intended to reach Jesus.

The Bible says, "She came up behind him and touched the edge of his cloak, and immediately her bleeding stopped" (Luke 8:44 *NIV*). After 12 long years of nonstop hemorrhaging, her blood flow suddenly came to an end. The power of God working through Jesus healed her instantly!

Persistent Faith Is Praised and Rewarded by the Lord

This passage goes on to say:

> **And Jesus, immediately knowing in Himself that power had gone out of Him, turned around in the crowd and said, "Who touched My clothes?" But His disciples said to Him, "You see the multitude thronging You, and You say, 'Who touched Me?'"**
> **— Mark 5:30-31**

Isn't it interesting that there was a "multitude" touching and thronging Jesus, but there is no record of anyone receiving healing except for this one woman. Why is that? How could all these people touch Jesus and not be healed? Because they weren't *believing*.

This woman with the issue of blood had a laser-focused faith. She kept believing and kept saying, "If I can just touch Him, I'm going to be healed." In her mind, Jesus was her only answer, which is what drove her to get to Him. The others in the crowd weren't believing in this way.

Once her blood flow stopped, Jesus knew that power had gone out of Him, and the Bible says:

> **And He looked around to see her who had done this thing. But the woman, fearing and trembling, knowing what had happened to her, came and fell down before Him and told Him the whole truth. And He said to her, "Daughter, your faith has made you well. Go in peace, and be healed of your affliction."**
> **— Mark 5:32-34**

Notice that Jesus didn't say, "Ah yes, because of My great power, you are healed." There was no arrogance or self-importance in Jesus' response. Instead, He immediately focused on the woman who was afraid and trembling. In addition to speaking peace to her heart, He also called her *daughter*, an endearing term that Jesus used very few times in the gospels. After calling her "daughter," He then praised her for her strong faith.

The Greatness of God's Power Is Coming Toward You

More than likely, there is something you need Jesus to do in your life or in the life of a loved one, and you are believing Him for a supernatural touch in that area. If Jesus was standing in front of you, what would He say about your faith in that situation? Could He praise your faith concerning healing as He did this woman with the issue of blood who was made well? Could He say your faith for finances has unlocked His provisions in your life? Or could He say your faith has caused you to become a more peaceful and loving person?

These are all good questions to ask yourself. One thing He would *not* do is focus on Himself. Instead, He'd focus on you. If you have laser-focused faith like this woman who was healed of the constant flow of blood coming from her body, He would say, "It's because of your *faith* in My mighty power that your prayer is answered!"

Friend, God's mighty power is relentlessly coming toward you! It's just looking for a faith-filled place to land. Is that you? Are you the one saying, "Lord, I believe. Please forgive me for doubting and being fearful. I choose to believe in You and Your Word."

When you open up your heart to the Lord like that, you open up a place in your heart to receive from His mighty power! That's His will for your life — He wants to impart His power to you! That's why Jesus paid the price, because He wants to touch you, deliver you, and heal you. Even now while you're reading this lesson, His power is coming toward you.

Ephesians 1:19-21 declares:

> ... **The exceeding greatness of His power** [comes] **toward us who believe, according to the working of His mighty power which He worked in Christ when He raised Him from the dead and seated Him at His right hand in the heavenly places, far above all principality and power and might and dominion, and every name that is named, not only in this age but also in that which is to come.**

Whatever problem you're facing, whatever name it has, God has put it under Jesus' feet. Receive from the power of God right now, whatever you need, in Jesus' name!

STUDY QUESTIONS

Be diligent to present yourself approved to God, a worker who does not need to be ashamed, rightly dividing the word of truth.
— 2 Timothy 2:15

1. If you have questioned or struggled to believe that physical healing is still available to you today, know that it is! Hebrews 13:8 says, "Jesus Christ is the same yesterday, today, and forever." So what He *did* He is *still doing*. Take time to look up and reflect on these verses concerning the healing power of Jesus that's available to you.
   • It's God's desire to heal you: Third John 2; Psalm 103:1-3.

- Obedience to God releases His healing: Exodus 15:26; Deuteronomy 7:15.

- The "stripes" Jesus received in His body paid for your healing: Isaiah 53:5; First Peter 2:24.

- God's Word brings healing — Psalm 107:20; Proverbs 4:20-22.

- Healing is received in Jesus' name: Mark 16:17-18; John 14:13-14.

2. There's likely something you need Jesus to do in your life or in the life of a loved one. What are you believing Him for right now? What promises from Scripture are you holding on to and speaking out loud over your life and your situation? If you don't have any scriptures, use a Bible concordance or an online Bible search engine to find and write down related verses you can stand on and speak out loud in prayer.

PRACTICAL APPLICATION

**But be doers of the word,
and not hearers only, deceiving yourselves.
—James 1:22**

1. Imagine you are the woman with the issue of blood. You've been suffering for 12 years, you've spent all your money on treatments, and your condition is worse not better. You've also been labeled by society as unclean and confined to live in isolation. How do you think you would respond to and handle such circumstances? What struggles and challenges do you think you might face? Would you be motivated to seek Jesus?

2. Denise said God showed her things in her heart that needed to be dealt with before she received the manifestation of her healing. Is there anything in your heart that shouldn't be there? Are you holding on to offense and unforgiveness toward someone you need to forgive? Has unbelief and doubt blocked God from moving in your life? Take a few moments to pray and ask the Holy Spirit to show you what's going on in your heart. Repent of any sin He reveals, ask for and receive His forgiveness, and ask Him to bring healing to your life.

TOPIC

What Can Faith Do?

SCRIPTURES

1. **Mark 2:1-12** — And again He entered Capernaum after some days, and it was heard that He was in the house. Immediately many gathered together, so that there was no longer room to receive them, not even near the door. And He preached the word to them. Then they came to Him, bringing a paralytic who was carried by four men. And when they could not come near Him because of the crowd, they uncovered the roof where He was. So when they had broken through, they let down the bed on which the paralytic was lying. When Jesus saw their faith, He said to the paralytic, "Son, your sins are forgiven you." And some of the scribes were sitting there and reasoning in their hearts, "Why does this Man speak blasphemies like this? Who can forgive sins but God alone?" But immediately, when Jesus perceived in His spirit that they reasoned thus within themselves, He said to them, "Why do you reason about these things in your hearts? Which is easier, to say to the paralytic, 'Your sins are forgiven you,' or to say, 'Arise, take up your bed and walk'? But that you may know that the Son of Man has power on earth to forgive sins" — He said to the paralytic, "I say to you, arise, take up your bed, and go to your house." Immediately he arose, took up the bed, and went out in the presence of them all, so that all were amazed and glorified God, saying, "We never saw anything like this!"

2. **James 4:8** — Draw near to God and He will draw near to you. Cleanse your hands, you sinners; and purify your hearts, you double-minded.

3. **Psalm 103:1-3** — Bless the Lord, O my soul; and all that is within me, bless His holy name! Bless the Lord, O my soul, and forget not all His benefits: who forgives all your iniquities, who heals all your diseases.

4. **Isaiah 53:5** — But He was wounded for our transgressions, He was bruised for our iniquities; the chastisement for our peace was upon Him, and by His stripes we are healed.

5. **John 10:10** — The thief does not come except to steal, and to kill, and to destroy. I have come that they may have life, and that they may have it more abundantly.

SYNOPSIS

Your anchor in the storms of life is your faith in the power of God and in His Word. It is a persistent faith we saw displayed in the life of both the Canaanite woman and the woman with the flow of blood. In this lesson, we will see this same strong faith demonstrated in the lives of four individuals who brought their friend to Jesus to be healed.

The emphasis of this lesson:

Four men literally took the roof off a house to get their afflicted friend to Jesus. Seeing their great faith, Jesus forgave the man's sins and healed him, proving to the scribes and the world that forgiveness of sins and healing are both made possible through Christ.

Four Men With Great Faith Brought Their Friend to Jesus

As was His custom, Jesus continued to move throughout Galilee, teaching the crowds and healing the sick. The Bible says, "And again He entered Capernaum after some days, and it was heard that He was in the house. Immediately many gathered together, so that there was no longer room to receive them, not even near the door. And He preached the word to them" (Mark 2:1-2).

Here we find Jesus in a house in Capernaum, and because the news of His healing power had spread far and wide, people came from all areas of the city to see Him and filled the house to the point that the people were spilling out the front door. It was crammed so tight that not one more person could fit inside.

The Scripture goes on to say:

> **Then they came to Him, bringing a paralytic who was carried by four men. And when they could not come near Him because of the crowd, they uncovered the roof where He was. So when**

they had broken through, they let down the bed on which the paralytic was lying.

— Mark 2:3-4

The actions of these four men display great faith. When they came up to the house and saw the huge crowd filling every square inch of floor space, they didn't say, "Now what are we going to do? We can't even get in the house to see Jesus. We can't tell Him our problem or get our friend to Him."

They could have easily given up and told their lame companion, "Well, it looks like we can't get in the house to see Jesus today. Maybe He will show up somewhere else tomorrow, and we can take you to see Him then." But that is not what they did.

Instead, these men decided that nothing was going to stand in their way of getting to Jesus. Looking around, perhaps their eyes caught sight of some steps leading up to the roof. Quickly, they made their way to the top of those steps and began tearing off the roof and lowering their friend down right in front of Jesus.

Now who would think of cutting a huge opening in a roof to gain access to Jesus? Only people with great faith. This should make us all stop and think, *What am I willing to do for my sick and troubled friends to get to Jesus? What lengths am I willing to go to so they can receive what they need from Him?*

These four men were willing to do whatever they could to get their friend to Jesus.

Jesus Saw Their Faith

Imagine the scene. A house is crammed with people standing everywhere to the extent that they are spilling out the front door. Everyone's eyes are locked on Jesus, and their ears are listening intently to His every word. Suddenly, bits of mud, straw, and small branches begin to sprinkle down from the ceiling just in front of Jesus.

As more and more debris begins to fall on the people, multiple sets of hands are seen penetrating through the ceiling, removing large chunks of the roof. Eventually, four men become visible and next to them is a fifth man on a stretcher. Once the opening in the roof is wide enough, the four men fasten a rope to the edges of their friend's bed and lower him down in front of Jesus.

How did Jesus respond to the actions of these men? Mark 2:5 says,

When Jesus saw their faith, He said to the paralytic, "Son, your sins are forgiven you."

Notice it doesn't say that Jesus saw the clumps of debris falling from the ceiling or that the crowd was in wide-eyed awe at the roof being torn open. It says that Jesus saw *their faith*. These four friends so believed that Jesus could heal their companion that they took to tearing open the roof of the house so that their friend could be restored to health.

Jesus Saw the Greater Need in the Paralytic's Heart

The first thing Jesus said was, "Son, your sins are forgiven you" (Mark 2:5). Now some might think, *The lame man's sins were not the problem. The fact that he was crippled was the issue.* But Jesus saw past what was happening on the surface and He saw into the man's heart. He knew what the man had done and was possibly even aware of the guilt he was carrying. Maybe the man couldn't receive healing because he felt unworthy to be healed. Whatever the case, the first thing Jesus said to him was, "Son, your sins are forgiven you" (Mark 2:5).

Many of us want a miracle or healing to occur in our life. We want God to operate in our life, or in our family's lives, or in our finances — but we're not willing to seek the Lord about what's in our own heart that shouldn't be there. Jesus knows what's in each of our hearts and wants to help us deal with it.

James 4:8 says, "Draw near to God and He will draw near to you...." When we draw near to God, He draws near to us with His power and the answers we desperately need. Therefore, when we are in an overwhelming situation that seems to be overtaking us, rather than just crying out for a miracle or healing, God wants us to draw near to Him so He can help us get to the root of our problem.

We see in this example of the paralytic man that was brought to Jesus by his friends that the Lord saw into the man's heart and forgave him.

The Hearts of the Scribes
Were Also Visible to Jesus

Now when Jesus told this paralytic man that his sins were forgiven, it caused no small stir among the religious leaders. The gospel of Mark makes this clear, telling us:

> **And some of the scribes were sitting there and reasoning in their hearts, "Why does this Man speak blasphemies like this? Who can forgive sins but God alone?" But immediately, when Jesus perceived in His spirit that they reasoned thus within themselves, He said to them, "Why do you reason about these things in your hearts?"**
> — **Mark 2:6-8**

Please note that the scribes *never spoke a word*. Their objection to what Jesus had said and done was voiced internally — it was what they were *thinking*. The Bible says that Jesus immediately perceived in His spirit what they were reasoning. In other words, He read their thoughts! Just as He knew about the sins in the heart of the paralytic that needed to be forgiven, Jesus could also see the unbelief and dishonor in the heart of the scribes.

Jesus Knew Why He Came to Earth

Keep in mind that as Jesus was speaking here, He knew exactly what He had been sent to do. He was mindful of the mission the Father had given Him to pay the price for mankind's sins by dying on the Cross. Jesus knew that He had been sent to bear both our sins and our sicknesses in His body, to descend into hell, and to rise again on the third day.

No one knew God's Word better than Jesus. As "the Word made flesh" (*see* John 1:1,14), Jesus knew Psalm 103:1-3, where David declared:

> **Bless the Lord, O my soul; and all that is within me, bless His holy name! Bless the Lord, O my soul, and forget not all His benefits: who forgives all your iniquities, who heals all your diseases.**

Jesus' assignment was to "forgive all our iniquities (sins)" and "heal all our diseases." Hence, He had the right to say to the paralytic, "Son, your sins are forgiven you" (Mark 2:5).

Jesus was also familiar with all the prophecies regarding His first coming, including these words spoken by the prophet Isaiah:

But He was wounded for our transgressions, He was bruised for our iniquities; the chastisement for our peace was upon Him, and by His stripes we are healed.

— Isaiah 53:5

As you carefully read this passage, you see that it says Jesus was "wounded for our *transgressions*," "bruised for our *iniquities*," and "the chastisement for our peace was upon Him." In other words, Jesus took the punishment for our sins upon Himself. Anything that would take our peace came upon Him, and by His stripes we are also healed in our bodies.

Forgiveness of Sin and Healing Are a Package Deal

Looking back at Mark's gospel, we can sense Jesus' frustration with the scribes because of what they were thinking in their hearts. He addressed their thoughts by posing this question to them:

Which is easier, to say to the paralytic, "Your sins are forgiven you," or to say, "Arise, take up your bed and walk"?

— Mark 2:9

Essentially, Jesus was saying, "Do you think it's easier for Me to forgive this man's sins or to heal him? To Me they are one and the same, and I'm going to prove it to you."

Again, Jesus knew that He didn't just come to forgive sins. He had also come to heal the sick. So, in Mark 2:10 and 11, as He stood before these scribes, He said to them:

"But that you may know that the Son of Man has power on earth to forgive sins" — He said to the paralytic, "I say to you, arise, take up your bed, and go to your house."

Forgiveness of sin and healing for our body are a package deal. The shedding of Jesus' blood and the sacrifice of His body took care of all unforgiveness of sins and all sickness and disease that would ever come against our body. Therefore, with the same measure of faith that we believe Jesus with for our eternal salvation, we should use that same measure of faith to believe Him for our physical healing. In addition to Him being our Savior, He is *also* our Healer.

God Wants To WOW Us With His Wonders

This amazing display of Jesus' healing power and forgiveness all started with four friends who wanted to see their lame friend healed. When they had heard that Jesus was in a house nearby, they came together and devised a plan to get their friend to Jesus. Not even the massive crowd could prevent them from getting him to the Master. They simply climbed to the roof, dug a large opening, and let their friend down in front of Jesus.

Their faith was speaking loud and clear, and it opened the windows of Heaven for God to do an amazing miracle. We see in Mark 2:12 that after Jesus told the man to arise:

> **Immediately he arose, took up the bed, and went out in the presence of them all, so that all were amazed and glorified God, saying, "We never saw anything like this!"**

Friend, God wants to show up and do things through our faith in such a way we are amazed and filled with wonder. The Bible calls it *signs* and *wonders*, and it means when we see miraculous signs, we wonder, *How did this happen? I don't understand it.*

As God puts His great power on display, He wants us to stand back and say, "Wow! This is a wonder!" That's exactly what happened with the paralytic man that day, and those who saw it said, "We've never seen anything like this in our lives!"

When Jesus does a miracle or heals someone like He did for the paralytic man, in His compassion and love He gives us our life back. He said in John 10:10, "The thief does not come except to steal, and to kill, and to destroy. I have come that they may have life, and that they may have it more abundantly."

If you're dealing with sickness in your body, what the devil stole through fear and torment, causing you to spend excessive money on doctors and treatments and experience sleepless nights and great frustration, Jesus can turn around in one moment, defeat the devil, and *give you your life back!*

STUDY QUESTIONS

Be diligent to present yourself approved to God, a worker
who does not need to be ashamed, rightly dividing the word of truth.
— 2 Timothy 2:15

1. The four friends of the paralytic man demonstrated great faith by
   their perseverance in getting that man to Jesus so he could be healed.
   What are some ways you can build your faith so it is strong for whatever need you or your loved ones may be facing? Study the following
   scriptures and get them deep in your heart so you can also demonstrate great faith when a situation arises.

   • Remember that God is faithful — Psalm 37:3; 40:10; 89:1.

   • Feed your faith — Romans 10:17; Second Timothy 3:14-17;
     Philemon 1:4-6; Jude 20.

   • Stay with the promise — Romans 4:20; Second Corinthians 4:13; 18.

   • Demonstrate your faith — Galatians 5:6; Second Thessalonians 1:3;
     Philippians 1:27; Colossians 2:6-7.

2. Jesus perceived what was in the heart of the scribes and knew their
   thoughts. The Bible says, "The heart is deceitful above all things,
   and desperately wicked; who can know it?" (Jeremiah 17:9). There's
   only one way to know what is in your own heart. Do you know how?
   Explore these eye-opening passages for the answer!

   • What do all these verses say about the hearts of all mankind —
     including *yours*?
     See First Chronicles 28:9; Psalm 44:21; Jeremiah 17:10; Acts 1:24;
     Romans 8:27.

   • What do these verses say God does to your heart and mind?
     What does He use to do it?
     See Deuteronomy 8:2; Psalm 7:9; Proverbs 21:2; Jeremiah 12:3;
     Hebrews 4:12.

   • What does God say is going to happen based on what's in your
     heart?
     See Jeremiah 17:10; 32:19; Revelation 2:23.

   • Take what David prayed in Psalm 139:23-24 and make it a person-
     alized prayer of your own.

PRACTICAL APPLICATION

**But be doers of the word,
and not hearers only, deceiving yourselves.
— James 1:22**

1. The four friends we learned about in Mark 2:1-5 were willing to do whatever they could to get their paralytic friend to Jesus. Stop and think, *What am I willing to do for my sick and troubled family members or friends to get to Jesus? What lengths am I willing to go to so they can receive the truth and supernatural encounter they need from Him?* Do you have someone in your life who needs a touch from the Lord? What is the Holy Spirit stirring in your heart about how you can help that person? What actions is He prompting you to take?

2. Take time to carefully reflect on Jesus' words in Mark 2:9-12 along with Isaiah 53:5; First Peter 2:24; and Psalm 103:1-3. What is the Holy Spirit showing you through this teaching regarding the forgiveness of sin and physical healing? How is He expanding your understanding of all that Jesus paid for through the sacrifice of His body and blood?

LESSON 5

TOPIC

How Can You Get to Jesus?

SCRIPTURES

1. **Ephesians 1:18** — The eyes of your understanding being enlightened; that you may know what is the hope of His calling, what are the riches of the glory of His inheritance in the saints.

2. **Mark 10:46-52** — Now they came to Jericho. As He went out of Jericho with His disciples and a great multitude, blind Bartimaeus, the son of Timaeus, sat by the road begging. And when he heard that it was Jesus of Nazareth, he began to cry out and say, "Jesus, Son of David, have mercy on me!" Then many warned him to be quiet; but he cried out all the more, "Son of David, have mercy on me!" So Jesus stood still and commanded him to be called. Then they called the

blind man, saying to him, "Be of good cheer. Rise, He is calling you." And throwing aside his garment, he rose and came to Jesus. So Jesus answered and said to him, "What do you want Me to do for you?" The blind man said to Him, "Rabboni, that I may receive my sight." Then Jesus said to him, "Go your way; your faith has made you well." And immediately he received his sight and followed Jesus on the road.

SYNOPSIS

So far in our study, we have seen the amazing things that happen when people approach Jesus. We saw how the Canaanite woman worshipped at Jesus' feet and how her persistent faith provided deliverance for her demon-possessed daughter. We also learned about the woman with the issue of blood whose laser-focused faith enabled her to get through the crowd so she could touch the hem of Jesus' garment and be healed. And in our last lesson, we examined the story of a paralytic man whose four friends took the roof off a house to bring him in front of Jesus. Their great faith resulted in a great healing miracle for their friend.

In this final lesson, we will explore the remarkable story of a blind man named Bartimaeus. Although he was well known as a beggar near the city of Jericho, his life was totally changed when he met Jesus!

The emphasis of this lesson:

Faith is a place. When we put our faith in God, trusting in His Word and in His power, we enter the place of faith. As we wait for the promise and grow in our faith, the Holy Spirit brings us into the place where we experience the answer we have longed for. Blind Bartimaeus moved from the place of his problem into the place of faith and received his sight — the answer he longed for.

A Revelation of Jesus Delivers Us From the Devil's Deceptions

So many believers have a head knowledge of Jesus, but they lack a heart revelation of who He really is. They believe Him to be their Savior and Lord, but they don't have a deep knowing that He is also their Healer.

We saw in our last lesson that forgiveness of sin *and* healing are a package deal in Christ. The shedding of Jesus' blood and the sacrifice of His body provides forgiveness of sins and at the same time takes care of all sickness and disease. Therefore, with the same measure of faith that we believe Jesus for our eternal salvation with, we need to use that same faith to believe Him for our physical healing.

Having a revelation of who Jesus really is sets us free from all the lies of the enemy and deceptions of our carnal mind. That is why the apostle Paul prayed, "That the God of our Lord Jesus Christ, the Father of glory, may give to you the spirit of wisdom and revelation in the knowledge of Him, the eyes of your understanding being enlightened..." (Ephesians 1:17-18).

Friend, God wants your eyes to see more than what you can physically see. He wants you to see with the eyes of the Spirit through faith into the realm of the spirit and understand what He can do. God wants to touch you and transform you with His mighty power. That is what He did in the life of a blind man named Bartimaeus when the man encountered Jesus near the town of Jericho.

Bartimaeus Was Known as a Blind Beggar

On one particular journey, Jesus and His disciples went in and out of the town of Jericho. History reveals that Herod the Great built a winter palace there and turned that area into an oasis of sorts. We begin reading in Mark 10:46, where the Bible says:

> Now they came to Jericho. As He went out of Jericho with His disciples and a great multitude, blind Bartimaeus, the son of Timaeus, sat by the road begging.

Notice that Jesus was with His disciples and a great multitude, and as they came into Jericho and later left that city, they saw a blind man named Bartimaeus on the side of the road. He had been begging in that place so often he became like a fixture on the road. At that time, people like Bartimaeus wore special clothes that identified them as blind and as beggars. This gave them the right to be near the street and beg in public.

On that day, Bartimaeus did the same thing he did every other day of his life — he got up and got dressed in the clothes that identified he was a beggar, and he made his way to his usual place on the side of the road. There he sat waiting for people to have mercy on him and give him money. The people in society had grown so accustomed to seeing him that when they passed by him, they would have subconsciously thought, *Oh, there's blind Bartimaeus. He's sitting where he always sits to beg every single day.*

But something was very different about the day Jesus passed by him. It was a day like no other day in the life of blind Bartimaeus. Mark 10:47 says:

> **And when he heard that it was Jesus of Nazareth, he began to cry out and say, "Jesus, Son of David, have mercy on me!"**

The fact that Bartimaeus cried out and kept crying out for Jesus to stop and help him indicates that he knew Jesus was his only answer. People don't start screaming out for someone to stop and pay attention to them if they don't believe the one they're crying out for is their only answer.

Faith Can Give Us a Brand-New Identity

Now as Bartimaeus kept yelling for Jesus' attention, the crowd started screaming back at him. Scripture says:

> **…Many warned him to be quiet; but he cried out all the more, "Son of David, have mercy on me!"**
> **— Mark 10:48**

More than likely, the townspeople were demeaning and said things to him like, "Oh, shut up, blind Bartimaeus! Just shut up and go sit in your corner like you do every day. We've known you all our lives. Just be quiet!" With each harsh insult they hurled, their words nailed Bartimaeus into his old identity as just a blind beggar by the roadside.

But in that moment when Jesus was passing by, faith came alive in Bartimaeus' heart! And that faith began to cry out for Jesus, the Son of David! Although the townspeople saw Bartimaeus as merely a blind beggar, faith was giving him a brand-new identity. That's what faith does. Others will see you one way, but when you see yourself through the eyes of faith and God's Word, you can take on a different identity in Him.

It doesn't matter what your mother, your father, your spouse, your teacher, your brother, your sister, or anyone else has said about you. Your identity is transformed when you see yourself through the eyes of faith and God's Word.

On that day, blind Bartimaeus didn't see himself as just a blind beggar. He saw himself through faith. He believed it was possible that the Son of David would have mercy on him and give him his eyesight, which would change his whole life. In just moments, Bartimaeus' expectations were about to be miraculously met.

Hold Tightly to Truth and Faith, Not the Opinions of Others

Again, Mark 10:48 says that the more the people warned Bartimaeus to be quiet, the more he cried out, "Son of David, have mercy on me!" He didn't care what the townspeople thought of him because Jesus was passing by, and this was possibly his only chance to get Jesus' attention. Thus, Bartimaeus kept screaming loudly, "Son of David, have mercy on me!"

Then suddenly it happened. The Bible says in Mark 10:49:

> **So Jesus stood still and commanded him to be called. Then they called the blind man, saying to him, "Be of good cheer. Rise, He is calling you."**

What is interesting is that the same people telling Bartimaeus to cheer up in Mark 10:49 are the same people who told him to shut up in Mark 10:48. These verses show us just how fast public opinion can change. One minute people like us and are supporting us, and the next minute or the next day, their feelings have changed and they're against us.

On that day, only two opinions didn't change — the opinion of blind Bartimaeus and that of Jesus. The crowd's opinion changed like the wind, which is the nature of all public opinions.

Let this serve as a warning to you to never give up your dearest and most precious convictions of faith because of the opinions of others. Always hold fast to the unchanging truth of God's Word. In other words, treat the opinions of others lightly and hold on tight to truth and faith.

Bartimaeus Believed for a New Identity, Telling Jesus Exactly What He Wanted

With Jesus now standing there and inviting blind Bartimaeus to come to Him, the Bible says:

And throwing aside his garment, he rose and came to Jesus.
— Mark 10:50

The fact that Bartimaeus threw aside his garment is important because the garment he was wearing was his *identity*. Remember, the clothes he had been issued gave him the right to beg. His garment gave him the entitlement to sit by the road, beg, and receive money from others. It was his way to make a living. By throwing it aside, he was throwing away the most important thing he had.

The only reason Bartimaeus would throw his garment to the side was because he believed he wasn't going to need it anymore. He believed with all his heart that Jesus, the prophesied Son of David, was going to have mercy on him and give him back his eyesight.

In Mark 10:51, the Bible goes on to say:

> **So Jesus answered and said to him, "What do you want Me to do for you?" The blind man said to Him, "Rabboni, that I may receive my sight."**

Jesus knew Bartimaeus was blind and wanted his eyesight, so why would He ask him, "What do you want Me to do for you?" Because Jesus wanted to hear it coming out of Bartimaeus' own mouth, "I want to receive my sight."

Friend, it's vital that we have honest conversations with Jesus. When we get in His presence and He asks the question, "What do you want Me to do for you?" He expects us to answer honestly. Unfortunately, most of us haven't spent enough time with God to know with absolute certainty what we want. But if we will spend time with Him in His presence, He will begin to open our understanding and show us things about Him and about ourselves we've never seen before.

God has given you special gifts and responsibilities, and the assignments of how to use those gifts will be made clear as you spend time with Him. What He reveals will also make clear exactly what you need Him to do for you.

Bartimaeus knew he wanted Jesus to give him his eyesight, so that is exactly what he asked for. And the Bible says, "Then Jesus said to him, 'Go your way; your faith has made you well.' And immediately he received his sight and followed Jesus on the road" (Mark 10:52).

The Place of Faith

Scripture doesn't say how long Bartimaeus had been blind, but we know his blindness was definitely a problem that kept him confined to a place of begging. As Jesus was passing by him on the road, faith came alive inside Bartimaeus' heart, and he cried out for Jesus' attention. He chose to believe Jesus had the power to heal him, and everything could change for the better with one touch from Jesus.

That was Bartimaeus' place of faith, which was a real place in his heart. Although the townspeople around him were trying to evict him from his place of faith and shut him up, blind Bartimaeus knew what he wanted and needed. Faith was in his heart to be healed, and that was the place he chose to stand. When Jesus finally called Bartimaeus and he stood before Him, Bartimaeus knew exactly what he wanted.

Friend, moving into a place of faith is a very real process. Since God sees the end from the beginning (*see* Isaiah 46:9-10), He sees you in your present stormy place of problems, but He also sees you in the place of faith. It's a place where you say, "God, I'm not moving from here. You've made promises to me, telling me who I am and who You are, and I'm not moving from here."

If you stay in the mental arena, the place of figuring things out and trying to understand everything with your mind, you're going to lose. Likewise, if you stay in the emotional arena, following your feelings and the feelings of others, you will miss out on the place of faith. But if you will focus on Jesus and the presence of the Holy Spirit who's living on the inside of you, you'll move into a place of faith and receive the answer you need and long for.

Yes, the problem is real, but the place of faith is just as real — and so is your answer from the Lord. If you will stay in that place of faith, eventually the mountain of problems will move, and you will come into the place of having God's answer. That's your destination — getting the answer to prayer you need and realizing that Jesus really is who He says He is and that He loves you more than words can say!

STUDY QUESTIONS

> Be diligent to present yourself approved to God, a worker
> who does not need to be ashamed, rightly dividing the word of truth.
> — 2 Timothy 2:15

1. Bartimaeus had heard of the amazing things Jesus was doing, and he believed that Jesus could do a miracle for him too. His faith gave him *a brand-new identity in Christ*. Likewise, when you see yourself through the eyes of faith and God's Word, you can adopt a brand-new identity in Him. Take time to meditate on these promises from Scripture declaring your new identity in Christ Jesus!

   • I am a _____ in Christ
     (2 Corinthians 5:17).

   • I am the _____ in Christ Jesus
     (2 Corinthians 5:21).

   • I am made _____ with Christ and
     _____ (Colossians 2:13).

   • I am made _____ in the Beloved,
     Jesus Christ (Ephesians 1:6).

   • I am God's _____
     (1 Corinthians 3:16; 6:19).

   • I am *not* _____ in Christ Jesus
     (Romans 8:1).

   • I am _____ in Jesus, the Head of all
     principalities and powers (Colossians 2:10).

   • I am blessed with _____ in the heavenly
     places in Christ (Ephesians 1:3).

   • I am _____ through faith in Christ
     (1 Peter 1:5).

   • I am _____ in both Jesus and the
     Father's own hands (John 10:28-29).

PRACTICAL APPLICATION

But be doers of the word,
and not hearers only, deceiving yourselves.
—James 1:22

1. Is there a "blind Bartimaeus" in your life? Is there someone you've seen so many times in the same place and in the same burdened, conflicted condition that you just tune them out as part of the everyday scenery? Who is it? Could it be that God wants you to bring hope and healing to that person? Pray and ask the Holy Spirit to tenderize your heart to be sensitive to His leading and to be ready to minister to this person when He creates the opportunity to do so.

2. When Bartimaeus heard Jesus was passing by, faith came alive in his heart. He believed it was possible that Jesus would have mercy on him and give him his eyesight. Bartimaeus' faith gave him a brand-new identity. Jesus is passing by YOU right now! He is your only hope for change. What do you need Jesus to do in your life? Cry out to Him and allow the faith He's placed in your heart to give you a brand-new identity in Him!

A Prayer To Receive Salvation

If you've never received Jesus as your Savior and Lord, now is the time for you to experience the new life Jesus wants to give you! To receive God's gift of salvation that can be obtained through Jesus alone, pray this prayer from your heart:

Jesus, I repent of my sin and receive You as my Savior and Lord. Wash away my sin with Your precious blood and make me completely new. I thank You that my sin is removed, and Satan no longer has any right to lay claim on me. Through Your empowering grace, I faithfully promise that I will serve You as my Lord for the rest of my life.

If you just prayed this prayer of salvation, you are born again! You are a brand-new creation in Christ! Would you please let us know of your decision by going to **renner.org/salvation**? We would love to connect with you and pray for you as you begin your new life in Christ.

Scriptures for further study: John 3:16; John 14:6; Acts 4:12; Ephesians 1:7; Hebrews 10:19,20; 1 Peter 1:18,19; Romans 10:9,10; Colossians 1:13; 2 Corinthians 5:17; Romans 6:4; 1 Peter 1:3

Notes

CLAIM YOUR FREE RESOURCE!

As a way of introducing you further to the teaching ministry of Rick Renner, we would like to send you FREE of charge his teaching, "How To Receive a Miraculous Touch From God" on CD or as an MP3 download.

In His earthly ministry, Jesus commonly healed *all* who were sick of *all* their diseases. In this profound message, learn about the manifold dimensions of Christ's wisdom, goodness, power, and love toward all humanity who came to Him in faith with their needs.

☑ **YES, I want to receive Rick Renner's monthly teaching letter!**

Simply scan the QR code to claim this resource or go to: **renner.org/claim-your-free-offer**

Connect WITH US!